Candles
in the
Darkness

Richard Keith Carlton

PublishAmerica
Baltimore

First printing

At the specific preference of the author, PublishAmerica allowed this work to remain exactly as the author intended, verbatim, without editorial input.

ISBN: 1-4241-5839-7
PUBLISHED BY PUBLISHAMERICA, LLLP
www.publishamerica.com
Baltimore

Printed in the United States of America

Candles
in the
Darkness

House of Many Rooms

In my house are many rooms...

A room of dreams,
wherein is found the essence of
who I wish to be.
For a man's dreams define him,
while his life's work may not.
In this room can be found old
poems, pieces of music, art,
empty bottles of cheap wine,
dusty old books read
time and time again.

A room of the soul,
where I cry out to God and
await His reply,
offering up my prayers,
my worries and my fears.
A space filled with old icons,
writings of a spiritual sort,
plaster statues, old Bibles,
hand worn rosaries
and frayed holy cards.

A room of shadows—

where are stored the darker things:
death, failure, regret,
locked tightly and well-guarded,
its key tucked safely away.
All contents stored in boxes;
little tombs of painful memories,
covered with sheets of white;
shrouds to hide the decay,
closed to all viewing.

A room of desire—
walls lined with prints and pictures
of old flames and lovers,
some weeping and some laughing.
Here are love's lost mementos:
locks of hair, bottled perfume,
various articles of lingerie,
crumpled sheets of paper—
tear stained letters of lament
and lovesick lines of poetry.

A room of reality—
no trimmings or trappings here,
nor plush carpet or paint.
Unadorned and simple but for
a single large mirror,
that wherever I may saunter
or what room I wander into,
or mood might possess me,
I see myself as I am.
This is my least favorite room.

A room of hope—
waiting to be filled with peace
and good things yet to come;
things that may not be possible,
yet seem attainable.
Decorated with the promise
of happiness and contentment,
painted in wishful colors;
soft hues of faith and resolve,
with large windows to the future.

A room of the heart—
where I spend most of my days.
The center of my house.
Here are found my dearest treasures;
the thoughts of my children
and sweet memories of their lives,
filled with sweet aromas of
who they are and what they have become,
their trials, triumphs and beliefs
and their wonderful gifts to me.

In my house are many rooms...

of light and shadow,
of the joy, gladness and tears
through countless minutes, hours, days
and nights that shape a life.
Listen to the whispers of the past
echoing through its hallways.
Though it may seem a bit cluttered
or filled with so many useless objects
and perhaps not to your liking,
please know you are always welcome.

Requiem for a Poet

He watched smoke rings rise into the air,
drifting slowly upward like some gray
ghostly figures searching for a haunt.
The acrid smell of tobacco filled the room
of his sad reveries like incense at a funeral.

The midnight hour of his journey in prose
had come upon him like a thief in the night;
stealing any semblance of inspiration.
He tightly gripped the pen in his weary hand,
waiting for the sweet whispers of his muse.

But at this hour, sluggish thoughts waded
through his scattered mind like a thousand
wandering pilgrims through quicksand.
Words formed like colors in a kaleidoscope.
He struggled to pen even one sensible line.

The pad of yellow paper sailed through the
dimly lit room of his frustration and struck
the clock which hung upon a barren wall.
He buried his head in his hands in a gesture
of irritation and complete surrender to the void.

A thousand words of verse flowed through his mind
in a flurry of chaotic imagery and tangled reveries.
He curse the Muse with hideous obscenities,
cursing the powers of art, music and prose.
In a moment of rage, he set fire to the pages

of his many words of fantasy, gloom, life and death!
Watching the flames engulf his room in a fiery pyre,
turning every word written from his heart to ashes.
Then raising his arms to the heavens in a mock prayer,
he flung himself into the flames…

Land of Shadows

In the land of shadows
dark rivers flow
in a gray forest deep,
in the valley of the souls.

In the land of shadows
no light dares to shine.
Trees stand dry and bare
and dreams are left behind.

Darkened clouds of anguish
forever paint the sky,
covering barren fields
where hope is left to die.

In the land of shadows,
place of broken hearts…
there, in a sightless fog,
is where all sadness starts.

Child of Dreams

The touch of death came early in his life.
Mid-September, a little place called,
Fredericktown...

Under a gray canvas canopy he listened
as a preacher said mournful prayers for
his father...he was four years old.

Though he didn't understand at the time,
the cold hand of sorrow had touched him
and would leave invisible fingerprints
to haunt the hours and days of his life.

He became a child of dreams...
lost in a world of fantasies and visions.
Hour after hour he would create images,
words and music to fill the empty days.

As the years flew by, he became scattered
like a lonely leaf blowing in the wind.
Without the guidance of his father,
he became lost in a fog of indecision.

Love came and went leaving scars that
would remain with him all of his days.
But through every heartache and with
every disappointment, peace always came...

in the beautiful dreams he held deep within,
for there lie his heart and his soul.
Wonderful words and music filled the
dark and lonely nights of his world.

It was in the wonderful images of his mind
that he would find rest and comfort to bear
the mediocrity and monotony of his days.
For no one can take away another's dreams.

The child of dreams, became a man of dreams.

She of the Truest Heart

She was a soft breeze blowing
life into a cold and lonely place.
Her love was of the truest kind.
There was no malice in her;
no deception in such a spirit
of pure and trusting love.

Her words were whispers of life
to a damaged and cautious soul.
A shadow of mystery creeping
across the walls of my heart,
she stole into my dreams with
her wounded eyes of tragedy.

To touch her for a moment,
I would have crossed many rivers.
To feel her soft kisses in the night,
I would have walked through fire.
Her memory holds a sacred place
in the cold rooms of my regret.

To speak her name to another
would be to desecrate the only
true love I have ever known.
She will forever remain a secret.
Someday perhaps she will return
and touch my life once again…

she of the truest heart.

Ship of Fools

I am the Captain of this ship of fools
and should you decide to book passage,
let me assure you, I am an old salty dog,
experienced in the moods of the ocean.
Though I shall charter a course for us
toward the golden shores of paradise,
we may sail through many a storm.

Let us raise the main sail now and set off
on our long and perilous journey of life.
For on this voyage of unknown adventure,
we will drift upon the mysterious tides of
worry, fear and doubt before we reach
our final and rewarding destination.
Feel the winds of time sweep us away.

And although this old vessel has endured
a thousand hazardous crossings in its history,
it has weathered many a raging tempest.
So do not fear the journey of a lifetime,
but stand at the rail and see the beauty
that stretches out across this great expanse
and breathe in the sweet air of freedom.

Stillness of Night

In the stillness of the blessed night
a certain, beautiful peace comes
upon the weary traveler...
gently soothing whatever wayward
thoughts may wander into frightened
hallways of the restless mind.

Through the quiet hours of evening,
peace intrudes upon the harried life
like a thief creeping in the dark...
urging a lonely, troubled soul
to be still and to hold on
until the tender light of dawn.

In the final hours of night
the debris of a busy day
is discarded for a brief time...
while the mystery of a deep sky
calms every useless worry or fear,
giving us hope for the new day.

The Beautiful Night

Oh, the beautiful night—
a billion shining eyes
lighting an endless sea,
as a tranquil moon floats
silently across the heavens,
watching over our dreams.

Between twilight and dawn
the darkness covers us
in a cloak of stillness,
blanketing a worn out world with peace,
while night birds sing soft lullabies
to quell our raging thoughts.

Through this soundless calm,
poets pen a thousand words
while lovers share kisses
and a legion of somnolent artists
fill lifeless and wanting canvases
with hues of their visions.

Oh, the beautiful night!
Do not fear its shadows,
for it offers no harm,
but rather a tender and quiet strength
to its many world-weary children
tired from the harried day.

Going Home

This train I'm riding
is taking me home again.
I have strayed so long
down the highways and
byways of indecision.

Across fields of destruction
have I wandered in vain.
In desolate valleys
I have spent my days
in shadowed seclusion.

I will walk again the paths
and back roads of my youth.
Where each day brought wonder
and my nights were spent
dreaming under the stars.

I have booked passage
on the train of redemption,
going home once more
to that place of peace,
before it is too late…

before the lonely nights
harden my tender heart
and the hope of love
dies a tragic death
of disenchantment.

Blow that lonesome whistle,
set these wheels in motion.
Roll me down the tracks
to my destination;
at last, going home.

Winter's Dream

I had a dream of a cold winter's morn,
walking down a snowy pathway
alone and forlorn.
Icy trees swayed from a brisk northern wind.
while in frozen silence I thought of
our love once again...

the warm summer days of our lovers' dance,
beneath a billion stars of dreams
all filled with romance.
I could hear the sweet songs sung in the night;
two kindred spirits sharing the hours
into the dawn's light.

Then came the sad sound of autumn's refrain,
bringing a cold chill to my heart
and then came the rain.
It poured down upon us in sheets of tears
to drown our sweet love in a pool
of suspicion and fear.

In my winter's dream I could see you there,
sitting on a snow covered bank,
wind blowing your hair.
You rose to greet me with a tender smile
and kissed my cold, trembling lips
and we danced awhile...

there in the snow like two children at play,
like two old familiar lovers
who had lost their way.
I awoke from my dream in a blissful way,
as the sun poured through my window
the light of summer's day.

Unfinished Music

Unfinished melodies play softly in my mind.
Things left undone, things never to be,
haunt the morning hours of my reveries;
tragic tunes of tempestuous times.

A song of unrequited love, wafts gently
through the empty spaces of my time.
Grace notes, unattended, neglected,
remain lifeless and soundless forever.

Bass keys thunder sad, mournful dirges,
as minor keys dominate my woeful hours.
Melancholy melodies of misty mornings,
provide the background airs of morbidity.

Remorseful requiems of loved ones past,
darken the rueful hours of remembrance.
And the music, unfinished, cries out to
the cryptic composer to be completed.

Through a Forest Deep

Towering giants, reaching to the sky,
with mighty arms outstretched,
swaying softly in the morning breeze.
They whisper, they sigh...
the trees.

A silent spirit blows thru my mind,
touching me, guiding me.
It cools fires of anguish within,
with a gentle gust...
the wind.

Above me, a swirling haze of gray,
peaceful pillows of comfort,
cover me in a blanket of calm
sprinkling teardrops...
the clouds.

Down a weathered, worn and beaten path,
I hear their fluttering wings
as they flitter thru the dense forest,
singing sweet songs...
the birds.

Resting my weary bones I sit awhile
beside a crystal clear
well of cool, refreshing water,
cleansing my tired mind...
the stream.

An oasis of wondrous beauty,
filled with images of life.
A place of quiet solitude
to hide from the storm…
the forest.

Keeper of the Stars

Keeper of the stars light my world.
Cast your shining brilliance threw
the gray clouds of my emptiness.

From the realms of reverie
send down showers of peace
to calm my restless days.

You are my one true lover
and keeper of my anxious thoughts,
my wondrous mystical muse.

The many years of my wandering
have left me vacant and tired.
Restore to me the power of love.

Shine brightly, my star light lady,
the glowing presence of life
and light my lonely rooms.

Blow away lingering shadows
with your sweet words of prose
and the breath of your spirit.

Shine, shine into my dreary days
a shower of hopes and dreams,
my saving and wonderful lover...

keeper of the stars.

Fredericktown

I can still smell Mama's apple pies.
Sitting out on the front porch,
counting every star in the sky.
And Daddy's old blue Plymouth;
its smell of smoke and living,
of living hard and tough.

Back when my heart was young and bold
and days spent in boyhood dreams;
visions forgotten by the old.
Running thru fields like a wild deer,
chasing down the billy goats,
racing the wind without fear.

Angelina, my first taste of love.
For me and that little country girl
life seemed never to have enough.
Young passion burning like a wildfire,
quenched only by love's sweet sighs,
exhaling all our sweet desire.

Maybe someday I'll head back down.
Who knows what I might find,
in that sad, sleepy little town?
Where my Daddy lies sleeping.
Where Angelina stole my heart
and willows are always weeping.

Fredericktown, oh sweet refrain,
many times I've sung your song
through the sunshine and the rain.
A melody of simple times,
ever written upon my heart
and forever in my mind.

On a Walk

Dawn has found me unable to sleep—
    nothing to do but walk.
Through gray city streets I make my way
    beneath a milky sky of chalk.
While the living dead in silent streams
    play out their mournful roles,
Hunger wastes their weakened flesh
    as terror grips their souls.
Near a garbage can a starving mutt
    picks at a rotting bone.
In a doorway filled with passion's treats
    two desperate lovers moan.

On and on I trek waiting for the muse
    to fill my empty mind.
A thousand words roll through my brain,
    but I can't pen one line.
So in vain I walk these desolate streets
    of loss and silent pain,
Among the tortured creatures of fate;
    gaunt faces dark and wane,
Perhaps to find in this wash of souls
    some twisted inspiration.
Or if truth be told to sate my own
    quiet desperation.

Through a sobering rain I set my course
    returning to safe haven,
Along avenues of hopeless yearning,
    past homeless and craven.
There to nestle in my comfort zone of
    boredom and simple dread,
Scribbling these heartless strokes of prose,
    sanctifying the dead.
At last to complete this masterpiece of
    profundity so deep.
Then close my mind, my heart, my soul
    and quickly fall to sleep.

Letter to My Father

We really never had time to know one another.
Your memories are like snapshots in my mind.
The color of your eyes or the sound of your voice,
have been lost to me but for imagination.

The cold black and white images left behind do
not reveal the heart or the spirit of you
and yet, I have always felt your presence;
certain scents and impressions steal upon me.

You have spoken to me in my dreams, dear Father,
always gently comforting me with your words.
But in my everyday life and through my whole life,
how I have missed the guidance you could have given.

So I write to you now, not with words, but the heart,
to tell you Dad, that although I can not touch you,
a son's love for his Father, in thought or in word,
is something even death can never take away.

Old Books

Old books are the best books.
Their covers worn and tattered
from years of use and sometimes abuse.
Their pages, yellowed a bit from time;
dog-eared from hands and fingers
of those who have passed thru them.

People revisit old books.
Sometimes they sit idly on a shelf,
collecting dust, of no interest to anyone.
But then some curious soul
rediscovers their true worth.

No longer fresh as when new,
when pages were crisp and unsullied.
But after time and many readings,
like an old and treasured friend,
one knows they can be trusted.

And sometimes they remind us
of who we were or places we've been.
They can make us laugh or make us cry,
with tales of wonder or woe,
and matters of the heart.

So if you find an old book,
lying there alone on some shelf,
blow off the dust and open it.
Turn the pages carefully,
reading ever slowly.

Let its words sink down deep.
And listen as you journey thru it.
For though the cover may be worn,
its pages a bit shabby,
always remember that...
old books are the best books.

Sad Old World

Stars are shining bright tonight from heaven.
A yellow moon keeps smiling down at me.
Pine trees look like giants in the moonlight.
and how beautiful this sad old world can be.

Nights like this I wonder if God's watching.
I wonder if he ever thinks of me.
I wonder if he sees his lonely children
and how beautiful this sad old world can be.

Weeping willows, morning dew,
distant thunder, sky of blue.
All of our daily troubles cannot be compared
to the beauty of this tired old world we share.

A gentle breeze has crept into the evening.
It whispers soft, a lullaby to me.
It tells me not to worry, God is watching
and how beautiful this sad old world can be.

Old Poets Like Me

What is to be done
with old poets like me?
Too old to rock and roll,
or for youthful reverie.

Shackled to the past,
living day to day.
Longing for a dream
that gently blew away.

Penning mournful poems
long into the night,
to captivate the souls
so damaged by the light.

Perhaps the musing
is what keeps us sane;
the lonesome lines of verse
or the dismal refrain.

A blessing or curse,
this thing poetry
fills the empty hours
of old poets like me.

The Last Dance

A great tempest swept over the plains—
a spirit wind, breathing life
over the land.
Songs were sung by maidens and chiefs,
while young warriors danced to the rhythm
of the moon.
Prayer flames reached up to the sky,
like flickering fingers hoping to
touch the stars.
In the distance thunder shook the earth,
mixing with the beat of the drums—
they were coming.

Little Foot watched her father, Red Hawk,
as he painted his face in the
colors of war.
The devils would soon be there and
the rivers of life she had known would then
flow with blood.
A cloud of red dust could be seen
and the iron-clad hooves of horses
could be heard.
The end or the beginning was near
and the plains would be littered in
bodies of death.

The great wind howled with a mournful sound
as the warriors screamed out with rage
and blind fury.
Scorching flames crackled and hissed as if
they knew their burning hot tongues
would blaze no more.
Red Hawk led his precious little daughter
over a small hill where they sat
beneath an oak.
He held her trembling hand and gazed
into her dark eyes filled with her fears
and he whispered.

"Little Foot, the end is near for us.
The devils who come will bring our
destruction.
The memory of our lives here and
the spirits of our people
buried in dust.
You must go across the plains of sadness
into a land you do not know,
but go you must.
Do not be afraid, my precious one,
your father's heart and spirit will
lead you on."

Red Hawk held his daughter close to him,
hoping to give her his strength and
his power.
She did not question her father's words
for Red Hawk was a great chief and
filled with wisdom.
Instead she fought back her tears
gazed bravely into his dark eyes
one last time.
Then slowly turned and walked away
from Red Hawk heading east toward
the black river.

Behind her, in the distance she could
hear the sound of drums in the wind—
the spirit wind.
As she approached the river she turned
and watched her father join the warriors
and the maidens.
To the north the dust cloud of death
brought the devils closer and closer
to her people.
With her heart and spirit she watched
the proud and brave as they shared—
the last dance.

The Bog

He found himself seated on
a black, decaying stump of
a tree, now many years dead,
not remembering why or
how he happened to be there.
His brogan-shod feet only
inches from the scum-coated
murky waters of a dark pool.

Surrounding him were bare and
ghostly trees that stood as so
many sentries in the gloom
against the pale, hazy light
of a thoughtless yellow moon,
while clouds of various hues
swirled round and across the
faceless celestial orb.

Whispers floated on a breeze
blowing softly through the
dismal and damp chilly marsh,
singing sad lullabies of lament.
Closing his tired and aging eyes,
he allowed the weight of
his troubled life of woe and
worry to crush down upon him.

He had come there many times,
but then only in a dream
that haunted him throughout the
dark, lonely times of sadness.
But he would not be waking now,
nor did he really care.
There in the quiet desolation
of the bog he would find his peace.

Dream Land

It's a place somewhere beyond,
somewhere I can't seem to find,
locked in some attic of time,
never to be seen or heard from.

There is always laughter there
and love so pure and giving.
The sky is continuously blue
and no clouds pass over.

Every word spoken is true.
Everyone you meet a friend.
There is no sadness allowed,
nor is there a need for it.

And a garden so beautiful
it would take one's breath away,
filled with only roses
that never wilt or bear thorns.

It's a place somewhere beyond,
somewhere away from this life.
What a pity it would be
if one had to die to get there.

Moon Dancer

She dances by the light of the moon
into the empty corridors of my dreams,
showering my delicate heart in a
wonderful swirl of moon dust.

I am lost in her sensuous shadows—
captivated by the glow of her beauty.
A rhythm of ageless innocence beats
softly in the light of a restless moon.

She is the healing spirit of love—
the midnight muse of my longing.
How did I spend my lonely hours
before she swept into my heart?

From a distant star in the cosmos
she dances away the quiet whispers
of loneliness, breathing new life
into the gray corners of my soul.

Moon dancer, dance with me tonight.
We will skip among the stars across
the beams of your sweet, gentle light
and cross the mountains of the moon.

Peaceful Morning

On this peaceful morning
you crept into my thoughts
as I awoke into the stillness
and quiet of it...

before the garish day
intruded into my life
with its rude remanding
and its mindless tasks...

into my twilight dreams
you whispered the purest of love
like a soft, gentle wind
with your sweet tender mercy...

Calm my foolish heart
and still my restless spirit
with your presence and love,
here on this peaceful morning.

Night Sky Dreams

I feel you here with me
in the stillness of dreams,
blowing soft kisses thru
the dark places of time.

In the stars you shine
like so many precious
diamonds in a black
sea of hope and wonder.

While night birds sing your song,
my lover, the moon, speaks
words of silent peace to me
from a sky of ebony.

As love overwhelms me,
I send a song across
the spaces between us
to touch your tender heart.

In the Wilderness

Through the desert of pain he trudges,
over dunes of destruction and arid
days of loss and isolation.
Like a shadow he crosses the land.
through the hot balmy nights
and ten thousand days of aimless,
hours of torturous wanderings.

But it was not always this way.
Once he had been the master of his world;
a warrior of great renown.
In the days of his valiant youth
he had slain the dragons
that so threatened his sanity
and dispelled the shadows of fear.

His sword was truth, his shield, justice;
courage and bravery, his bludgeons.
No man dared to challenge him.
And the maidens sought his attention
and the strength of his arms.
For his kiss was like a fire
burning with passion and pleasure.

Then came the years of discontent.
The clouds of war gathered in blackened skies
of malevolent conflict.
And his kingdom began to crumble
and he was defeated.
In humiliation he fled
to the wilderness of despair.

Now he roams this bare wasteland
in the solitude of his memories.
A dark and lonely figure,
a nomad, wandering the desert sands,
struggling for survival,
holding on to mortality.

Out of the Wilderness

From the great plains of sadness
he emerged at last ...

The sultry winds of mourning,
etched upon his worn face
a thousand lines of pain.
Weathered by loss and regret
over burning sands of time,
healed now in hope's sweet rain.

Behind him, long weary days
of restlessness and fear,
spent wandering in vain.
Ahead, a river of dreams,
waiting to quench his thirst
and wash away his pain.

There in the distance he saw,
a mountain of peace and love
rising above the hot sand.
And through a forest of green,
someone was waiting;
waiting to take his hand.

To the land of dreams he traveled...
out of the wilderness.

Cold Morning

As I lay here in my bed,
a tangled sheet becomes a shroud
covering all my hopeless thoughts.
This dreary solitary cell
feels as empty as a tomb.

Through my window I watch
a lonely grackle carelessly
swing on a telephone wire;
my only companion unless
he crashes to the ground.

Perhaps the sun may shine again
and if so, who would notice?
Angelus bells are tolling
in a somber melody surreal,
on this cold and lifeless morn.

The Early Hours

Here in the early hours,
in a peaceful silence,
between midnight and dawn,
faded and near forgotten
memories come stealing into
my drained, weary mind.

Memories of lost things,
people, places and dreams
cross the chasm of time
to tread uninvited the bare,
cold hallways of my mind
ever so freely.

And unable to sleep,
I yield to their presence
with some feeling of dread
and hesitant surrender,
cursing my insomnia,
with no place to hide.

These useless intrusions
of days long ago past
are like yellowed pages
of an old and worn out book
that no one reads collecting
dust upon a shelf.

Yet I entertain them,
hoping they will quickly
dissolve into my dreams
and leave no trace behind
of guilt and cruel regrets
to haunt my waking.

The past is never dead
as long as the minions
of memory invade
our thoughts and hours
like so many unwelcome,
boorish visitors...

in the early hours,
between midnight and dawn.

Fields of Clay

In fields of clay my brothers lie...
beneath the tall thin grass
of the plains of sorrow

Warriors of a time far away...
when skies were filled with the
spirits of the sun

Arapahoe and Shoshone...
Cherokee and Comanche,
Kiowa and Apache

Sons of thunder rolling across
the wild deserts and hills
of pride and tradition

Mighty children of the good earth...
fathers, sons and brothers
of the heavens and stars

Their fate sealed in blood ambition...
dreams and visions scattered
upon the four winds of hate

Now laid to rest in final peace...
beneath the tall thin grass
in these sacred fields of clay.

For Natasha

You came to me one night,
telling me how you loved
the words I scribbled on
the pages of your heart.
And yet, your words of
sweet and dark poetry,
swept a blue light of wonder
into my mind and thoughts.

I have never read or felt such
sadness and passion in all of
the thousands and thousands
of words my eyes have seen.
In that cold place in the north,
where the cold rivers flow,
you warmed my heart as no
other before you or since.

My love, my dear Natasha,
your broken life bled thru the
cracks of my shattered heart,
inspiring me to be the man
I always knew I could be.
You shared your pain and
the tender parts of your soul
and touched mine with love.

I would have forsake all that
I have or ever will have to
cross the frozen rivers of
your torment and slay the
dragon who haunted you.
I would have opened the steel
gates of my heart to let you in;
would have loved you...

But I became reckless in my
prose and penned some lines
of venom against a dark maiden;
lines you thought were for you.
And you vanished into the night,
never to be seen nor heard from.
The loss of your tenderness led
me to seek the solace elsewhere...

into the arms of a capricious and
cold black heart of deception...
And now, after all these hours,
after the loss of your love and
your sweet inspiration, my heart
is a leaf blowing in the wind.
No matter if I should love
ten thousand times in my life,
there will always be the sad,
mournful memory in my heart...

of Natasha.

I Wonder

I wonder…
where are you
in the spring of life
when dreams are clouds,
wafting aimlessly
across indigo skies
while love dances
in fandango twirls…

in autumns' bare morns
when colors turn pale
into shades of gray mist
painting the sky in harsh
gray longings
threatening the day…

since winter has come
with merciless cold
and its cruel vengeance
suffocating last gasps
of wishes
that never come true?

I wonder…time
where are you?

Sleepwalker

Through the many years and miles,
in the realm of dreams and wishes,
I have walked in a waking sleep.

In my endless nights of roaming
I searched for peace and reality
among the dreams of despair.

Like a man walking in a
continuous fog of confusion,
I longed to be awakened.

Scattered images so surreal
haunted the hours of my time
in vague shadows and whispers.

Until at last, I awakened
with a dull sense of purpose,
weary from my sleepy travels.

I began to walk and breathe
in the daylight hours of my
quiet, but simple existence.

Across the Sea

Somewhere, across the sea of my dreams
there is a place of peace at last.
From this shore of my wandering heart,
I gaze across uncertain and restless tides.

Though this ship of fools I sail upon
has veered at times from its course,
I know I am in the hands of a capable
and trustworthy, seafaring Captain.

Perhaps beyond the distant horizon
someone stands gazing on another shore.
One day they may board this ship of fools
and sail with me across a sea of dreams.

Along a Crooked Road

Somewhere on your journey
the pathways became unclear.
You lost your way among
the tall grass and thickets
obscuring your direction.

And you found yourself there
standing on a crooked road
of loss and indecision,
unable to take another step
for fear of stumbling further.

Alone, surrounded by
dark forests of ominous
and dangerous misfortune,
you called out to anyone
for the help you so needed.

But no one has come and
your fear and hopelessness
increases with each passing day.
And you continue to walk,
for it is all that you can do.

I want you to know that although
I cannot walk the path for you,
I will be there at your side
no matter where the road leads
and to what end it may come.

You are not alone on this
treacherous trail of adversity.
I will go the distance with you,
for I have walked down
many crooked roads myself.

Morning Poem

The old poet sat silently in thought
in the early hours of morning,
candle light flickering,
quill in hand,
an empty parchment
lying lifeless before him...

And he began to write of love
and the passion and pain of it,
recalling memories,
bittersweet,
hours spent longing,
matters of the heart...

Years swept by him in clouds of
mournful gray and of purest white,
soft kisses through the night,
sad goodbyes,
the joy of first love
and bitter tears of regret...

A single drop of rain trickled
down his world-weary face upon
the scribbled prose before him,
as he paused
unable to pen
another dismal word or line...

But a poet's heart never stills,
whether in joy or in sorrow.
The poems must be written,
in the night,
in early morning,
through calm and tempest...

And so he continued to write
an ending to his morning poem,
through the tears
and the memories
sweeping over him,
of love's passion and pain.

A Poet Dreams

A poet dreams
and a thousand maidens dance,
as he paints his prose
with visions of romance.

A poet smiles
and our troubles fade away,
gray skies turn to blue,
the dark night turns to day.

A poet weeps
and legions of angels cry,
while in pain he pens a
melancholy lullaby.

A poet dreams
and opens another door,
showing a weary world
the way to dream once more.

A poet dies
and a thousand words take flight
across endless skies,
forever lost to night.

Evening Sonata

I hear the hum of traffic
through an open window.
A sonata plays softly from
another room, wafting towards me
as though carried by a breeze.

All unease flowing away,
as the sweet melody
cradles me in loving arms,
rocking me, slowly, gently,
as a mother would her babe.

The night brings no shadows,
only soft glows of peace
and a moment's silent repose,
as the garish day has now been spent
and becomes only memory.

Here, in the evening watches,
concerns dare not intrude
for the jealous spirit will
not allow the hour to be shared
by useless worries and fears.

And the music plays on,
drifting through silent dreams,
refreshing my tired body,
as though sent from heaven above,
to still a world-weary traveler.

The Dance Goes On

Feel the rhythm of your life
run through every waking thought.
It beats out the moods of time—
joy or pain, light and shadow.
For each life lived, is a dance.

We dance through the sad hours
of sorrow and loneliness,
through the hours of our joys,
through the unforgiving nights
and mornings of redemption.

We glide across our dance floors,
sliding and swirling in time
to the sound of distant drums
pounding out our life's tempo
through the sunshine and the rain.

And the dance of life goes on
through each day and each hour,
whether in love or in loss,
in the passion or the pain,
in swirling measures of time…

the dance goes on.

Angel with the Broken Wing

A cold and heartless wind
blows a frightful breath at me.
But I have no fear of it,
for there is an angel that
speaks to me through time
and across the miles of tears.

She understands my darkness,
she takes away the years of pain.
But she can not fly to me
on this dreadful, mournful night;
my angel of desire and hope,
my angel with the broken wing.

In another time and
so many dreams now past,
she was a maiden of light,
soaring high above the rain.
But a demon broke her wing
with his devilry and lies.

And she came then to rest
upon a cold, northern star,
tired, broken and abused.
Looking down from her exile,
she saw a weary, hapless soul
and sung to him a wondrous song.

Blow away, cold dark wind,
for I will not suffer you.
For I hear an angel's voice,
calling from a distant star.
An angel of love and of beauty,
my angel with the broken wing.

Dancing Spirits

You and I, two dancing spirits
across the wind swept days
of ecstasy and anguish,
will at last...be one.

At long last, our shadows
shall see the light of day.
The long eons of waiting,
finally...past us.

Let us fly through the heavens
on wings of sweet redemption,
and touch the stars of freedom.
You and I... dancing spirits

Desire

In the darkness of my desire
there lives a princess...
a sinister temptress of lust.
She has no face,
nor is she real to the world.
She is the seed of obsession;
seducer of men...like me.

The light, a burning fire to her,
for she dwells in shadow...
the shadow of my weakness.
She has no soul,
and her spirit, only mist.
She is a mistress of the flesh;
the object of my...passion.

She knows I can not refuse her
nor would I care to...
for I am only flesh and blood.
She frightens me,
but my fear fuels her.
She comes to me in my dreams;
beckoning to me...with eyes,

cold and black as a midnight sky,
drawing me into night...
the dark night of my longing.
She never leaves,
for she is a part of me.
That secret place of my mind;
the deep caverns of...desire.

Sunday Morning

How I long for you this Sunday morning.
Dawn's light is creeping into my room
as I stare through the window and wonder.

All is well in my little corner of the world,
yet I care little for anything these days
except for the thoughts I have of you.

There is a part of me always waiting
for a dark cloud to shadow the horizon.
Years of disappointment have left their scars.

And I know, if love should drift far away
upon the changing tides of indifference,
I will continue to live my simple life.

But life without you would be forever empty.
For you have filled my dreams with love
and the brilliant light of your many gifts.

How I long for you, my beautiful dreamer,
my beacon in the dark nights of loneliness
always guiding me to calm, peaceful waters.

So I will turn away from the clouds of doubt
that come with the cold, dreary dawn
and long for the beautiful night…and you.

Shadows and Whispers

tiny voices and images...
haunting shadows and whispers
a movement here and there
a wave of melancholy
slight tinge of gloom

they come

distorted truths whispered...
never believed yet still heard
flashes of harmful light
echoes of darker things
impossible

they are not real

in the still hours of morning...
in the dark watches of night
shadows and whispers
voices of ill intentions
nothing to fear

or is there?

Traveler

His old shoes are worn
from the journey.
His back tired and sore
from many miles.
Across burning deserts
and streets of gold,
from shores of wonder,
through deep valleys.

Over mountain peaks
and lazy highways,
Traveler has searched
long for his peace.
Past the sleepy towns
and great cities,
through emerald fields
has he ambled.

But in all his journeys
the peace he seeks
has not been found,
nor will it be.
For peace comes not
from miles of roaming,
but in each hour
spent in wisdom.

He only needs to
stop for a while
and rest his weary
body and mind,
to look around him
at the beauty
to be found in
in the place he dwells.

Across the Stars

I am boarding a rocket called Happiness
and heading into the cosmic skies of
Hope and Freedom.

Across the stars into the Milky Way
and past the black holes of Fear and Worry.
I am alive!

This old world has nothing for me now
so I am setting sail on cosmic ship
called Healing.

Traveling at the speed of Light I will
soar across the universe of Chaos
into a peaceful space.

Climb on board this vessel of freedom.
For I am headed beyond the mountains of the moon…
across the stars!

House of Dreams

I live in a house of dreams.
I have been here for many years,
wandering from room to room,
vision to vision, hope to hope.

Many dark nights have I spent
here alone lost in reverie.
Wishes have come and gone
with the changing of the seasons.

Once I dreamed of truest love,
when I was young and filled
with the wonders of the heart.
But for some dreams we must wait.

In every room of this house
is a memento of dreams past.
It is filled with many windows,
so I can look toward my future.

Throughout my house of dreams
you will see shadows and light.
It is painted in gray tones of pain
and rainbows of sweet redemption.

And if I should travel across
the world of sadness or worry,
I will always make my way home
to the place where my heart is…

my house of dreams.

A Thousand Miles

A thousand miles and a million
dreams to share...

I will come for you my dearest,
come on the strong winds
of my love.

Across burning deserts of fire
I will find a way
to your heart.

Time has no meaning for us,
for you and I are
timeless spirits.

No tempest of doubt or worry
can quell the power
of our love.

You are the center of my world
and I race toward
that center.

No my lover, a thousand miles
cannot hold me back
from my dreams.

Drifting

Over the hills of Dreamland,
through the Valley of Shadow,
beneath the Mountain of Hope,
he walks between dark and light...

drifting.

He is a man of many trials;
an enigmatic figure, wrapped
in the folds of the night.
Wandering through the
hollow canyons of his life,
seeking redemption, peace.

Fear has no place in him,
for he has fought the battles
of the world and the heart.
He travels the road of truth,
but too often alone on the path;
searching always for love.

His loves ever in abundance,
even if his heart should break.
Every man he meets is a friend,
but few ever know his thoughts.
His secrets remain a part of him
as he rambles across his life.

He was born of a bitter wind,
scattered through the hours
of his brief, but weary journey.
But forward he goes, ever hopeful,
for he has known light and shadow
and seen the changing tides while...

drifting.

On the Shore

How long had he stood on this shore,
eyes gazing across the deep expanse,
his feet covered in the hot sands of time?

Many the day he watched dim shapes
of passing ships on the horizon,
wondering where they may be going,

while the fickle tides of his fate
washed the cool waters of his hours
upon the shore of his discontent.

But on this day, tides were turning,
pulling out to sea his life's debris—
clearing the shore of useless waste.

Across deep waters of Providence,
beneath changing clouds of fortune,
a light shone upon the far horizon.

And the light came towards the shore,
casting shadows of regret behind it,
growing in brilliance as it approached.

Then, as if in silent prayer,
he opened his weary arms as
though somehow to embrace it.

The restless sea at once became still
and the tides of fate stopped turning
as the light approached the waiting shore...

it was the Light of his redemption.

I Remember Mama

I was thinking of Mama tonight...

I remember the night she died
I wept like a little kid.
My heart was so broken I
thought I'd never get over it.
Even as I write this little poem,
there is a lump in my throat.

I stood by her bedside that night
as she lay in a peaceful repose.
The worries of her world gone.
But also, the spirit and soul
had passed far away into that
place we all wonder about.

I sat in a hospital chair and
just looked at her lifeless frame.
And as the tears streamed down
my face, I saw something else.
I saw the woman that she was.
The woman who was my hero.

I remembered all the nights she
would work long and late hours
just to put food on the table.
And God, I remembered her smile.
I swear, it could light up a room
and did so many, many times.

I remembered that it was my Mama
who sung those old songs I loved.
She had a wonderful voice and could
whistle like a songbird in night.
She bought my first guitar for me
and some little five and dime store.

Hell, she probably couldn't afford it,
but she wanted me to play and sing.
You see, Mama always knew that I
had the heart and soul of a poet.
So many nights she would say to me,
"Richard, get your guitar and play."

And I remember Mama sorting beans
in her old worn flowered apron as
she sat at the kitchen table singing.
Now I'm telling you, brown beans
and cornbread have never tasted as good.
Hell, life has never been as good.

Quiet Time

Somewhere on a beach perhaps,
walking through golden sands
lost in simple thought, I may find
the peaceful quiet time that I seek.

When life's endless stream of noise
begins to clutter my busy mind,
I need to silence the raging din
that assails my imperfect world.

Life is filled with beautiful sounds
that fill the hours of our daily tasks,
orchestrated in ~   h and harmony
                              or.

                              unds

                    agitation,

                              less

Midnight

It is midnight...

I embrace this night of calm.
There is no fear of a darkness
that offers such hallowed peace.

I am alive, engulfed in the deep
shadows of its mindless beauty—
its warm cloak of tenderness.

By a single candle light
my mind takes flight upon
the wings of night's healing winds.

The black expanse of silence
cradles me in secret solace,
offering sweet, dark kisses.

Dawn may awaken me to
the light of my reality,
but my spirit awaits its master...

midnight

When I Get Home

When I get home someday
I want to see the valley;
green fields of clover
mixed with the dandelions
that never seem to die.

I wonder if old Jim
ever got that Chevy going.
Seems like he spent half
of his sixty years working
on that damned old thing.

Now that Mama's gone,
no need to visit the house
where I spent my youth.
Nor will there be a need
to walk thru her garden.

But I will visit the grave
and tidy it up a little bit.
It's the best I can do,
though it makes no sense,
at least I feel close to her.

Daddy, he's been gone some
forty-two years this May.
But you know, I still hear
his voice every now and then
calling me home for supper.

I heard Jeannie got married
to that dumb Hank Wilcox.
I swear, that man was so
stupid, he couldn't find his
way out of a cardboard box.

Guess it don't matter much,
he's got Jeannie and I got
nothing but useless memories
about a place far away and
ten million tears down the road.

Even so, I'll go on home someday
and walk around the town like
some haunting specter of gloom.
But hell, no matter what I say,
I just can't wait until I get home.

Rose of Gotham

There is a garden, north of Gotham,
where grows a gentle rose.
The scent of this tender flower
reaches across a thousand miles
filling my world with its fragrance.

Among indifferent weeds and vines
it stands tall and strong,
sending out a sweet aroma
whether in sunshine or rain,
arousing my sleeping senses.

For an old gardener like myself,
who has seen many petals
wither on the vine of apathy
and fall upon the soil of my heart,
this rose is a gift from heaven.

And someday soon I will travel
over long, winding highway
of all my hope and my dreams,
across a thousand miles of love
and find my gentle rose of Gotham.

No More Tears

I have cried rivers of tears
through many hours and years;
in the still of the night,
in the grip of my fears.

But the rivers have run dry
as I now let the past die;
for in the light of dawn,
the memories go by.

All the mournful shades of blue,
are painted in colors of you;
the soft strokes of your love
gentle touches of hue.

Walk with me through all my years,
through the valleys of my fears.
I promise you my love,
there will be no more tears.

Flowers

Like a flower in a garden,
the spirit within us
must be well attended.
Or like thorns among roses,
concerns of this world
may often offend it.

Should a careless gardener
not first work the soil,
his labors will be in vain.
His precious flower will grow
among sand and rock
and wither I the rain.

Let us begin to till the soil;
the ground of all our days,
removing each worthless stone.
For the spirit, like a flower,
requires special care
to reap what was sown.

Fragile Thread

Love, even at its best,
hangs by a fragile thread.
Distance and doubt haunt me
as I lay upon my bed.

Wondering where you are
and longing for your touch.
Thinking perhaps that love
demands a bit too much.

Is the pleasure it brings
worth any of the pain—
the moments of sunshine,
the hours of rain?

Perhaps the cloudy day
has brought me to this state.
Should I surrender,
leaving all to fate?

My poor heart has had it fill
with the burden of love.
No matter how much is given,
it never seems enough.

Love, woven by dreams,
hangs by a fragile thread.
How can such sweet emotion
cause a heart such dread?

Leaf Blowing

A leaf blowing in the wind
all the hours of my days.
From here to there with
each breeze along the way.

An unwilling voyager—
no direction or course.
Swept up by capricious gusts,
without thought or remorse.

Then came tumultuous gales,
spattered with dark debris
in the summer of my years,
tearing and scattering me.

Until at last I settled
in autumn's sweet mercy,
amid a quiet woodland
as winter sheltered me.

At last, awakened in spring
by the sun's soothing gaze,
with all my colors restored
to continue on my days.

Running Free

I guess you've trudged many a mile girl
across the plains of sadness.
I myself came flying down
riding a star of madness.

Two lifetimes separated
by cold tears of rain,
coming together
just to share the pain.

Your whispers float upon the breeze
above the moon's hopeless light,
"Ride fast across the stars,
come and fill this empty night."

Down through the hills I travel,
riding hard and long,
to the mournful melody
of a lost maiden's song.

Kindred spirits running free
across the gray fields of buried bones,
racing fast against the wind
from another hour alone.

Dawn's sweet light will soon appear
for the night is fading fast.
Two wounded hearts are we,
running from the past.

Icy Windows

As I stare through icy windows,
snow covers the world like a shroud.
And cold, lonely winds
swirl and chase about.

As the hours pass me by
like nameless strangers without care,
they remind as they go
there is little time to spare.

I long for warm wet kisses
on this frigid winter's night—
love's tender embrace,
the glow of its light.

But a season of betrayal
sowed bad seeds of mistrust
while the field of my heart
lies covered in dust.

Passing cars creep by
wheels muffled by the snow,
as I stare into a storm
through these icy windows.

The Old Man on the Bench

He sat alone on a park bench,
feeding pigeons small morsels of bread
from a white, crumpled sack—
wisps of white hair blowing in
the soft, gentle, summer breeze.

A picture of serenity, this small,
gray man of some seventy years.
His peaceful countenance
drew me close to him until
I joined him there on the bench.

We sat in silence for a while,
watching the birds as they each
took turns picking the scraps
the old man provided them,
until at last he spoke to me.

"How are you today young man?"
His voice broke the silence of
the peaceful moment, startling
me a bit and then I answered,
"Well, guess I got no complaints."

He smiled slightly, never turning,
"Everyone has a complaint son."
I found myself smiling at that.
"Yeah, well, I guess that's true,
but who really cares anyway?"

"I do," he answered, "I do son."
Now I turned slightly towards
the old man and looked at his
wrinkled, time-worn face and
saw blue-gray eyes looking back.

"Do I know you sir?" I asked.
His eyes never left mine, but
they were warm and tender eyes,
that almost glistened in the sun,
calming my troubled thoughts.

With a voice like a whisper on
the wind, the old man replied,
"Whether or not, I know you.
I know you are troubled by life.
I see a sadness in your eyes."

For a moment, I was stunned
and ready to voice my anger
at such a rude presumption,
but my ire was short-lived as
he continued to calmly speak.

"So many people are lost and
searching life for the wrong things.
They miss the beauty of it all.
Hours, days and years wasted
worrying their time away."

Then he turned to the pigeons
as though pondering his words.
I turned and stared at the ground
and said to him quietly,
"I don't think it's that simple."

"Yes son, it is that simple.
You have been wandering like
a man walking down a road,
putting stones in a sack
until they start to weigh him down."

"Then he complains and moans
that the burden is too heavy!
Put the sack down son, today!"
He finished abruptly and a
silence arose between us.

I was angered by his words
and I wanted to respond,
but something inside of me
understood the wisdom of
this small, peaceful man.

I turned again towards him
as he fed the little birds
and clearing a lump that was
rising up in my throat,
I asked him with all respect,

"Tell me then sir, what of the
man who for his whole life
has walked its roads gathering
every stone in his path—
who will help carry his burdens?"

He turned slowly to look at me
with those warm, tender eyes
that seemed to stare into my soul,
and with a soft, quiet whisper,
he said to me...

"I will, my son,
as I always have."

Painted Mask

He paints his face
in bright colors of merriment,
while his heart dwells
in shades of blue.

Dancing, he twirls
a rainbow tinted umbrella
as he runs through
the pouring rain.

When he falls down
people laugh at his misfortune,
but his heart aches
from the tumbles.

In the spotlight
of the moment he is the man
he has always
dreamed he would be.

Then the light goes out,
the bright colors are washed away
and the little clown
becomes a man.

We love the clown.
He helps us to escape from
the daily circus
that surrounds us.

We never care,
nor can we ever really know,
the face behind
the painted mask.

Bernadette

Bernadette…

What a pure spirit were you,
soaring across the miles
of your brief sojourn here
on wings of feathered fancy.

I dream of you so often.
Not in a worldly way,
but as one touched by
your gentle grace and beauty.

Your inspiration to me
cannot be expressed in
the simple words of
a simple and humble man.

An angel on earth were you,
a soft glow shining in
a dark room of shadows,
touching every life with love.

Sleep well, messenger of peace,
for your journey here was
filled with a suffering
only a saint could bear.

The Empty Hours

Last night I dreamed of you, Mother.
Almost ten years now, but
your precious memory grows
like a rose in the garden of time.

Oh, the empty hours my dear,
spent here without you as the
long days come and go like
swift clouds across the endless sky.

Say a prayer for us, Mother,
there from Heaven's gate, for
all of your lonely children
left here in this wasteland.

Someday soon we'll meet again,
high above the stars and
together fill each empty hour,
on the other side of time.

Reach Out

Reach out across the miles
that separate our dreams
and catch me before I fall.
Night winds sing such sad
and mournful songs to me,
like a tempting siren's call.

Even the stars above
seem to hold back their light
as I grapple with my fear.
Our moon veils his face
lest perhaps I may see
a sad and soundless tear.

The silence of the night
has muted the voice of love
in a black hole of musing.
The clarity of my thoughts,
once so focused and sharp,
are now jumbled and confusing.

Reach out across the sky
and hold my trembling hand.
Pull me back into your light,
before passing clouds blind me
to the beauty of the dream
and the hope of dawn turns to night.

Night Falls

Night has fallen
and creeping shadows
close fast upon me.
I pray, that with dawn,
they fade as a dream.

I awaken
beneath a sky of blue
and wait for comfort,
but comes a cloud
and with it, shadows.

I journey in darkness
as one lost in a valley
of endless fog.
The path of hope,
uncertain and steep.

My mind is weary.
Thoughts, like fallen leaves,
scatter into the wind.
A spirit once alive
now shrouded in gloom.

Where are you Light
that once shone with me
your tender mercies?
Do not forsake me now
to dwell in shadows.

Empty Cathedral

I walked into an empty cathedral,
my footsteps echoing off a
dull and dirty tiled floor,
where I chose a well-worn pew
and knelt down to pray.

A peaceful, hallowed silence stole into
blank and vacant mind,
calming a storm within,
until an old memory
slowly filled the void.

I closed my eyes in a cool surrender
letting the memory take shape,
with some trepidation,
afraid of what I may see,
yet knowing I must.

It was then I pictured a small boy
standing close by an open grave
in a country cemetery,
trying his best not to cry
on a gray, chilly morning.

A cold September rain fell steadily,
mingling with the little tear drops
that trickled down his face—
holding tight to his Mother's hand
struggling to be brave.

Then he whispered softly to his Mother,
"Why did Daddy have to die?"
But there was no answer given
and he never asked again
for the rest of his days.

Then I followed him through all of his years,
watching each season of his days
as I would an actor
on a stage playing the part
that life had given him.

Weeping through each sorrow he endured,
angered by every blow he bore,
longing to speak to him,
wanting to tell him that there
was another way.

Helplessly I watched as he faltered
under the weight of his burdens,
unable to help him
as his whole life fell apart,
leaving him broken.

I could bear no more so I opened
my eyes to escape the memory
and felt a sting of tears
trickling down my worn face
in hot streams of regret.

I rose from my aching knees and tread
once more upon that old tiled floor,
my footsteps echoing behind
me as I found my way out
into the cold night.

As I walked into the chilling air,
a shooting star fell from the sky
like a flaming arrow
aimed toward this sad old world
to a fiery death.

I gazed into an unforgiving sky,
my sad eyes tearing from the cold
gust of a September wind,
and asked a white cold-blooded moon,
"Why did Daddy have to die?"

Dance Salome

Dance Salome, dance
and free my cluttered mind.
Lure me into fantasies
sweet and so divine.
Unveil each certain pleasure
long hidden in the heart,
releasing all the demons
that would tear me apart.

Whisper to me dreams
of ever changing light.
Reveal to me, dark lover,
the treasures of the night.
Sway softly to the rhythm
of thunder's steady roll,
exposing all the pieces
of your passionate soul.

Come to me in silken
veils of lace and set me free.
Uncover shadows hidden
in secret parts of me.
I seek not your love
nor a childish romance,
but your wicked delights.
So dance Salome, dance.

Uninvited Guest

You are never far from me,
are you Mister Jones?
I hear you on my doorstep,
rattling those bones.

That wicked little cackle
gives me such a chill.
And disturbing my pleasure
gives you quite a thrill.

I guess that I should have known
you would make your way here,
dark bearer of doubt,
mad keeper of fear.

You always bring a shadow
wherever you go.
And an icy touch of gloom
to darken the soul.

While I was lost in a dream
you slipped thru a window,
like a thief in the night
bearing much sorrow.

I have grown weary of you
but this of course, you know.
I understand your tricks now,
so perhaps you should go.

Yet, is even for a while
you leave me alone,
you are never far from me,
are you, Mister Jones?

Dark Water

Black and unforgiving water
flowed beneath the bridge.
Icy cold currents waited
for the old man.

He had long a go ceased to believe
in anything at all.
Hopelessness had led him now
to the old bridge.

The dark water beckoned to him
promising final peace;
mindless, hypnotic deep
whispering lies.

The old man stared into a swirling
black whirlpool while an
aching down inside longed
for its coldness.

Too many dreams now forsaken
through the lonely years
and wishes left unfulfilled
prompted him now...

while phantom pools of deception
preyed on the old man's
desperate and gloomy thoughts,
luring him downward.

It was then a memory shone—
one dim light of hope,
shining for a brief moment,
into his mind.

But it was enough to turn him
from the dark water—
from the edge of the bridge
to one more day.

The water watched the old man go
with disinterest.
For the cold currents knew
others would come.

Useless Reveries

Dreams of fire and ice
that pervade my thoughts
with their fickle fancies
of endless contradiction,
are so much of a burden.

Mindless streams of useless
and futile visions
that dissipate with each
passing wind of musing,
leave me weary of it all.

Images of darkness
and reflections of
things that will never be
are wishes of a wayward
and misguided state of mind.

Oh, to clear the slate and
begin a new season
of clarity and lucid,
dreamless contemplation,
is at last my only dream.

Restless Musing

Words are elusive this night.
Feelings more than thoughts
inspire the muse.
Oh how meaningless
and so useless it all seems.

But something is stirring here,
some mournful desire
or fantasy,
waiting to take life
and yet somewhere beyond me.

My mind, an empty canvas,
waits for the oils of
inspiration
to be applied by
a skillful artist's brush.

But weariness has spoken
to my aching bones
and aging back.
So I surrender
to the indifferent night.

A Cry in the Wilderness

Alone I wander in this wilderness
of confusion, weariness and pain.
I cry out like a wounded animal,
but no one seems to hear me.

Breathing the hot air of regret,
roaming over dunes of empty
days and lonely, lonely, nights,
my words are lost in the wind.

Exiled here, like a criminal,
stranded in the sultry arid place
of nothingness, crying out!
But still help seems far away.

How long must I be punished
and imprisoned in the yellow
haze of this barren wilderness?
Each hour my heart grows faint.

The dreams of my youth are
buried deep in the hot sands
of lost memory and wasted days.
I am growing weary of it all.

Death of a Poet

The words always came to him,
but few ever understood
the price paid for such prose.

To open a heart to the world,
the poet must reveal all thoughts
whether of light or shadow.

But images must be painted
in vague colors and pale tones
of ambiguity.

Blank sheets were his pallets
and the sharpened quill his brush.
Black ink was his life's blood.

He had penned a thousand words,
with a thousand more to come,
but his passion was waning.

The Muse would whisper in his ear
memories and impressions
to guide his troubled mind.

But it was, at last, his heart
that rejected all inspiration.
The quill began to dull.

Hours turned into days
as his life's blood thickened
into a formless disinterest.

They found him at his table,
a blank sheet of white paper
crumpled in his cold hand.

He was laid to rest
in a field of gray stones.
On his tombstone these words:

"Here lies a poet's bones,
his life's blood now dried...
may his words die with him."

Enigma

How can a love so real and strong
turn into a nightmare of bitterness?
Two people share so many hours
in so many ways with each other,
only to become strangers...

or enemies.

How can lovers' kisses so warm
become as cold as a winter frost?
When the sound of their voice
thrills you through the dark nights,
how can love become...

a whisper?

She and I were players in a tragedy
of lost love and the death of its beauty.
To look in her eyes was to drown in
a sea of magical wonder and passion.
And now I can barely look at her at all.

She loved to hear my music and the sound
of my voice as I read her amazing poetry.
When she said the words "I love you,"
it would take my breath away...

now there is silence.

If I live one hundred years in this life,
I will never understand this enigma;
this senseless loss of love between two
kindred spirits joined in so many ways.
How can two lovers turn into strangers...

and enemies?

Magdalena Plays

She plays at night for me
when I am weary from life.
Sweet melodies from a time
so long ago and far away.

Her fingers touch each key
with the love of her craft,
softly caressing each air
like a lover in the moonlight.

Magdalena plays for me.
She knows the light it sends
into the gray areas of my heart.
And heals me with each note.

Play, Magdalena, play for me.
Make love with your fingers,
arouse my passion with your
melodies of unending love.

Lighthouse

The lighthouse stood alone
in a bare, frozen field of
winter

it had seen many years
and many people pass
by

stood the test of time
against the winds of
adversity

passing ships had come
and gone in a black sea
of time

gales and tempests had
rocked its walls with
fury

and though it was shaken
it did not fall down in the
storms

no one can say how long
it will last in the field of
life

but its light will shine thru
the fog and mist as long as
it stands

To Touch the Blessed Sky

Look at that night sky,
my God, it is phenomenal.
I am wrapped the clouds
so gray, yet so inviting.

They swirl as they pass
in a dark dance of love.
The trees appear as black
hands reaching to touch
the blessed, sky of tears.

There is freedom in pain;
a final release from the
grip of surrounding fear.
In pain, we let go of it.

Shades of gray paint the
holy sky of our suffering.
For in suffering comes a
sweet knowledge of truth.

I raise my hands in prayer
to the Artist who has painted
skies of many emotions.
I raise my thankful heart...

to touch the blessed sky.

Until Stars Fall

I will cherish you until the
stars fall from the sky.
When a black midnight sky
came to darken my world,
you shined a tiny light of
goodness and love.

You never asked about pain,
you only spoke of healing.
Reaching inside of my book
of dreams, you pulled out
the man behind the tears.

Now the black nights have
turned to deep purple tones
filled with the light of a
one single, shining star
to guide me thru the dark.

I will remember the words
of comfort and strength
you penned from a heart
of true friendship and love,
chasing my shadows away.

If knowing you is only a
brief moment in the days
of my journey in this life,
I will remember your light,
until stars fall from the sky.

Twilight

Somewhere between end of day
and night's beginning is…
twilight.

The moon creeps into the sky
as the sun fades slowly…
away.

Hours of toil are over.
A time for reflection…
and rest.

Soft breezes caress my thoughts
while a lone evening star…
twinkles.

Cares are cast upon the sea,
for now is the hour of…
twilight.

Lost Child

She will tell you what you want to hear...
show you the dark side of passion.
Sing to you through the nights of
endless delusion and whisper vague
words of love to bring you into her world.

Like a child, lost, you will be drawn to
the air of merriment and sensuality.
But you will be drained in the end of
every thing you hold dear in this life.
For she is a lost child...lost in shadow.

Through your window at night, like a
specter haunting your every move, she
will stalk you...follow you in your dreams.
You can not tame the little beast inside her,
but will be broken by her childish lies.

Be careful then, you who would search
for love in the far reaches of shadow land,
for she will seduce you with her eyes
and make you weary, wanting more of her.
But you can change her...this lost child.

After the Storm

In a black and stormy sky there is a dream being born;
a little patch of blue where the sky has been torn.
There is tomorrow when the day has been cold,
a happy ending when the story has been told.
And there's a rainbow... after the storm

Through the sorrow and tears are lessons to be learned.
There remain only ashes where the past has been burned.
There is forgiveness when a wrong has been done,
a just reward when the long race has been run.
And there's a rainbow...after the storm.

When the well runs dry, God sends a healing rain.
So don't worry about the troubles of the day.
And when cold winds blow storms into your life,
don't be afraid...there's a rainbow on the way.

For every day of toil, there comes a night of rest.
With whatever comes your way, you can only do your best.
For there is hope when this old road turns rough;
a quiet little place when you feel you've had enough.
And there's a rainbow...after the storm.

Beneath a Cosmic Sky

Beneath a cosmic sky tonight
I roam this city street.
Clouds dance in angry swirls
while thunder drums a beat.

Sirens scream in ghastly tones
as the dealers ply their trade.
People passing in a mist
where empty dreams are made.

I see young demons watching me
from the glow of a neon light.
I say, "Bring it on now demon boys,
cause I'm ready for a fight!"

"With a right fist full of love
and the other full of hate,
I'll send you all straight to hell
and leave you at the gate."

But they slip into the shadows
and my spirit passes by,
as a darkened orange haze
paints the lonely cosmic sky.

Cause they know why I have wandered
on these haunted streets tonight.
I've come to face these devils
and put my fears to flight.

Too long have I been troubled by
all their evil and their hate.
Time to even up the score
before it gets too late.

So I walk beneath a cosmic sky
filled with the ghosts of the past,
with a strong will and resolve
to be free of them at last!

Dance of the Muse

In my dreams and thru all of my hours
she dances...

In colorful veils of the rainbow
she dances through my mind.
Whispering songs of life and love,
caressing my troubled thoughts,
inspiring me to pick up the quill
and pen my many magical memories.

She speaks to of love lost, the passion
and pain of the heart's many journeys.
In dark reveries she holds my hand
as it scribbles the fears of the past.
Twirling ever in an ever flowing motion,
she taps out a rhythmic measures of prose.

The Muse, my true lover, never forsakes
or leaves me alone when dark nights descend.
She tells me tales of wonder and woe
all through the beautiful nights of peace.
I hear her song across the stars of heaven
as I join her in a mystical dance of prose.

Dream Catcher

When this old world tries to drag me down,
I reach up into God's open sky of hope
and I catch a dream...

Days drag along sometimes
like a worn out snail.
Nights seem as empty
as a hollow log,
But I don't worry anymore,
I have dreams to catch up on.

Skies turned a little gray
and it seemed the sun
may have lost some of
its brilliant light.
Then I woke up and remembered
I have a dream waiting for me.

Words flow through my mind
in an endless stream.
And music soothes me
through lonely hours.
So a few days of rain don't bother,
cause I'm going to catch a dream!

Forest of Light

Down on the back roads
of a timeless little town,
before discount stores
and super highways,
was a secret place.

It was tucked away
in a cold, gray hollow,
hidden by twisted trees
and guarded by angels—
a place of wonder.

The people called it
the "Forest of Light,"
though few ever saw it
or spoke of the Man
who wandered thru it.

But legend has it
he was a powerful Prince
of such great miracles—
a Prophet of dreams,
filled with visions.

And they say he was
raised from moon dust
and that in his eyes
one could see the end
of the universe.

And sometimes at night,
stars would dance across
a sky of deep purple,
while a choir of angels
sung songs of heaven.

And each spirit could find
an oasis of peace,
where war had no place
and every broken soul
was granted mercy.

But there came a storm.
From the depths of the
earth, a black angel
rose up from the abyss
and formed an army

of man-like jackals,
that entered into
the Forest of Light,
and killed the great Prophet
who wandered thru it,

spreading all evil
desires and perdition
along the back roads
and thru all the towns,
extinguishing the light.

But sometimes at night
in a sky of deep purple,
beautiful voices
can be heard upon
the winds of heaven.

I Dreamed of Purple Skies

Last night I dreamed of purple skies.
Beyond the clouds of doubt I traveled
into the black and peaceful realms of
space and a billions galaxies of stars.

I found myself in a garden of delight.
Peace swept over me and calmed the
tempestuous winds that had raged
inside my fragile and gentle heart.

There was a beautiful lady waiting there,
dressed in a purple gown of understanding.
She beckoned me to come closer to her
and I approached her beauty with no fear.

It was though she had known me all my life.
Her words spoken were like smooth wine
that flowed into the dry, empty places in me.
And I sipped this nectar from a cup of affection.

But soon, the dream began to fade into gray.
The cup of her sweet and tender attentions
slipped from my hand and fell into a void.
As her image disappeared into a ghostly mist,

I reached out to touch her loving hands but
her beautiful vision had slipped into darkness.
I awoke from this dream in disappointment.
For I had not opened my heart to her.

Let the Rain Fall

Let the rain fall down.
Let it wash away the
dirt of a thousand days,
a cleansing of the past—

showers of healing
and deliverance.
For the years have
sullied the spirits of

light and integrity,
leaving behind soiled
souls of jaded clay.
The joy of our youth

has been smeared with
passing hours of grime
from a dusty old world.
Let the rain pour down

an abundance of hope
upon the fallen children
of dreary doubt and despair,
washing away their sorrow.

Moonlight

Across the seas I feel your touch.
Moonlight fills my heart with you.
And the stars smile down on me
with eyes of twinkling delight.

The night sings a lullaby of
gentle and soothing peace.
Your voice sails upon waters,
drifting towards these shores.

A shooting star streaks toward earth,
like a heart falling in love,
as my lover, the moon kisses
my mind in tender passion.

I stand here on this lonely shore,
raising my hands to heaven,
giving thanks in joyful praise
for the night and the moon.

Mountains and Valleys

I have seen the view of life
from many mountains.
Looking out over a vast
hills of contentment.
In times of peace and joy
we must savor all of our
mountain top moments...

for life leads us also through
many days in the valleys.
Life looks somewhat different
looking through bare trees
of want, worry and strife.
But the hours spent in the
dark, cool valleys of life

are just as important to us.
For it is in the valley of tears,
that we take time to reflect.
Time to take account of all
the things pas or present,
that make up who we are
and who we wish to be.

But we must remain in the
cold gray mists of longing.
No. We must begin the
journey up to the mountain.
The path may be steep and
filled with thorns and bristles,
but climb we must...

for it is atop the great mountains
that we see where we have been
and where it is ...

we are going!

Song of a Night Bird

There came the song of a night bird
a quiet melody, yet enough to draw
me from a well of sadness.
The candle of sorrow burned bright
as I sat in the shadows.

From a distance I heard the song
of a heart so far, far, away from me.
And yet, it sung to me of hope
and its beautiful air spoke of life
rousing me from my dark thoughts.

I blew out the candle of sorrow
as the song of the night bird brought
new light into my soul.
There was no reason for sadness,
but a reason to live.

The gray specters of the past days
disappeared into black of night.
And I lit a candle of renewal,
its glow chasing away the gloom,
as the night bird sung its song.

The Death of Memory

Farewell you troublesome ghosts
that have haunted my many days.
I banish you to everlasting past;
to the shadows of lost reverie.
No more of your cold, sad refrains.

Too long have I tolerated you;
mournful memories of morbidity.
The grave of your sorrow has
been dug and awaits you now.
Future lights now shine for me.

I will drink a toast to your demise.
And light a candle for your soul.
But soon the dirt shall your home
and your spirit of despair, no more.
No flowers will I place on your grave.

Memory is dead…no more to rise
and disturb the days of my longing.
A fitting end to the longs days past.
I leave you now in solemn repose
to the empty void of what never was.

Words upon the Wind

I send my words to you…

from my damaged heart
into this sweet night of
purple light and dreams.

With pen in hand,
my words fall upon
the pages of the wind,
blowing across the
deserts of my musing…

to the one who inspires
me to live and hope
even in the creeping
shadows of my hours

may my humble prose
fall into your heart and
fill your hours with one
moment of peace

for all the times your
words of dark, beautiful
rhythm and rhyme have
quelled the storms that
raged inside of me…

I send my words upon the wind…

to you

Our Moon

Where is our moon tonight?
Yes, I see it now, smiling
down at me, like a friend.

The black sky holds me
close and comforts me,
as stars light up the sky.

And our moon speaks
to me of love and life.
And I sway slowly to

the symphony of this
dark and beautiful night.
And dream away the hours.

Oh my darling, my love,
forgive the words of a
damaged and broken soul.

Dance with me now
wherever you may be,
beneath the light of…

our moon.

Beyond the Clouds

Through the gray pillows
of passing tears, into a sky
of blue dreams I soar.

High above and beyond
every storm cloud of fear
I am lifted by gentle winds.

For, restless moments
of indecision and fog
cannot hold me here.

I have fared all seasons,
cold winters and springs
and know their changes.

So I will not linger
here in this valley below
for too much longer,

for the tides always turn
and there is always blue sky,
somewhere beyond the clouds.

Road of Light

I have been away too long...

long have I strayed from
the road of light that has
illuminated many dark
and weary days.

While I walked in the
sweet light of truth,
my way was clear
and my heart at peace.

But distractions of a
cold and fallen world
called to me and I
chose to leave the road...

the road of light that
had been leading me
to my redemption.
I chose the dark roads.

Into a forest unknown
I followed the darker
angels of my mind.
Until I was at last, lost.

But even then, I saw a
light in the darkness.
And I followed it,
stumbling many times

and giving up all hope
that I would ever find
the road of light again
that would lead me home.

But now, here I am,
bruised and broken
from my dubious travels,
limping along, once again...

the road of light.

The Burning

The funeral fires have been lit
and the dead bones of the past
set into the flames...

they are no more
than ashes blown
into the night wind

ghostly spirits
haunting specters
mere illusions

let the band play
mournful dirges
the choir is silent

your memory
a black page in
the book of death

smoke rises up
the last billows
of what once was

dawn approaches
the fire is gone
leaving only ashes...

from the burning

Redemption

He awoke to a distant song
coming through the window
of his troubled mind.
A cooling wind blew thru
his spirit ...something new.

He arose and walked the
little path to the cliffs.
In an orange painted sky
a voice entered his heart
in gentle whispers...

Below him he could see
the dark abyss of things past.
Across the plains in a mist
there came a soft glow of
light towards him...

Upon the far horizon came
quiet voices of angels,
singing new songs of hope.
And a word wafted like a
breeze into his spirit...

"REDEMPTION!"

Printed in the United States
63732LVS00002B/86

9 781424 158